★ THE CIVIL WAR ★

NORTH OVER SOUTH

Final Victory in the Civil War

by Michael Burgan

Content Adviser: Brett Barker, PhD,
Assistant Professor of History,
University of Wisconsin–Marathon County

Reading Adviser: Alexa L. Sandmann, EdD, Professor of Literacy,
College and Graduate School of Education, Health, and
Human Services, Kent State University

COMPASS POINT BOOKS
a capstone imprint

Compass Point Books
151 Good Counsel Drive
P.O. Box 669
Mankato, MN 56002-0669

This book was manufactured with paper containing
at least 10 percent post-consumer waste.

Managing Editor: Catherine Neitge
Designer: Heidi Thompson
Media Researcher: Svetlana Zhurkin
Library Consultant: Kathleen Baxter
Production Specialist: Jane Klenk
Cartographer: XNR Productions, Inc.

Library of Congress Cataloging-in-Publication Data
Burgan, Michael.
North over South : final victory in the Civil War / by Michael Burgan.
      p. cm.—The Civil War
 Includes bibliographical references and index.
 ISBN 978-0-7565-4369-3 (library binding)
 ISBN 978-0-7565-4413-3 (paperback)
 1. United States—History—Civil War, 1861–1865—Juvenile literature.
 I. Title. II. Series.
E468.B94 2011
973.7—dc22   2010001018

Image Credits: Corbis/Royalty-free, 5, 22, 25, 28, 38, 52; Getty Images/Hulton Archive,
cover; Library of Congress, 3 (all), 6, 8, 11, 12, 14, 17, 20, 27 31, 34, 36, 41, 47, 49,
50, 53, 55, 56, 57 (all), 63; North Wind Picture Archives, 43; White House Historical
Association/White House Collection, 45.

Visit Compass Point Books on the Internet at *www.capstonepub.com*

TABLE OF CONTENTS

CHAPTER 1
GRANT TAKES CONTROL

In late June 1863, Confederate troops marched from Maryland into southern Pennsylvania, an invasion that would end near the little town of Gettysburg. The rebels' clash there with Union soldiers would be a key battle of the long, bloody Civil War.

At the same time, hundreds of miles to the southwest, General Ulysses S. Grant and his Union forces were approaching the end of a long waiting game. The North had been trying—unsuccessfully—to take the important river city of Vicksburg, Mississippi, for months. Southern cannons there, set high on rocky cliffs along the Mississippi River, kept Grant's men away.

The North and South were now more than two years into the Civil War. The election of Abraham Lincoln as president in 1860 had stirred southern fears about the future of slavery. Lincoln, a Republican from Illinois, opposed the spread of slavery but said he would do nothing to restrict it where it already existed. Some members of his party, though, wanted to abolish slavery completely. Many southern slave owners did not trust the new president to keep his word. That fear prompted 11 southern states to leave the Union and form the Confederate States of America.

Lincoln said the states had no legal right to secede, but that made no difference. The Civil War began in April 1861 when Confederate artillery fired on Fort Sumter, in South Carolina, and the Union Army fired back.

★THE SIEGE OF VICKSBURG

As the war reached the Mississippi River, President Lincoln called Vicksburg "the key" to northern success. "The war can never be brought to a close," he said, "until that key is in our pocket." The North already held New Orleans; if Vicksburg fell, Union ships could freely travel the

Ulysses S. Grant became Lincoln's most successful general.

entire Mississippi River. In addition, Union control of the river would split the Confederacy in two, limiting the movement of soldiers, weapons, and supplies between the two parts.

Earlier in the spring of 1863, Grant had laid out his plan to capture Vicksburg. The northern troops would cross from the west side of the great river to the east, then move north to attack the city. In April Union ships dashed by the booming Confederate shore guns to reach Grant and ferry his troops across the river. By May the Union troops were closing in on their target. The Confederates tried to hold them off at several points, but the North kept advancing.

Grant had attended the U.S. Military Academy at West Point and fought in the Mexican War in the 1840s. He later

Union ships raced past Confederate soldiers firing from the bluffs above the Mississippi River.

left the Army, but when the Civil War began, he quickly asked to serve for the North. He first won fame in 1862 with victories in Tennessee. But now, as Union troops were nearing their target, Grant could not fight his way through the southern soldiers and artillery defending Vicksburg.

After a second failed assault on May 22, Grant began a siege. His troops prevented supplies from reaching the soldiers and citizens in Vicksburg, and his artillery blasted every day and night in an attempt to weaken the defenders' will to fight. A woman trapped in the siege wrote in her diary: "We are utterly cut off from the world, surrounded by a circle of fire."

As the weeks passed, food grew scarce, with some families eating little more than rice and mule meat. The Vicksburg newspaper had to use wallpaper to print the news, since the regular paper was gone. Union shells destroyed homes, forcing residents to seek shelter in their cellars. Even there, the shells rained down, leading to bloody wounds and death.

General John C. Pemberton led the Confederate troops in Vicksburg. He had decided to stay in the city when Grant first advanced, fearing he could not defeat or outrun him. During the siege, Pemberton hoped for reinforcements. By July 1 he knew he was trapped with no way of surviving Grant's siege. On the afternoon of July 3—just as General Robert E. Lee's Confederate

Grant accepted the white flag of surrender at Vicksburg July 4, 1863.

forces made their last charges at Gettysburg—Pemberton put up the first of his white flags. He officially surrendered the city the next day. Grant called the white flags "a glorious sight to officers and soldiers" who now believed "the Union was sure to be saved."

In the meantime, after suffering heavy losses at Gettysburg, Lee and his men were forced to retreat back into Confederate territory. Lee, the commander of the Army of Northern Virginia, was a respected general who before the war had loyally served the Union. But when his home state of Virginia seceded, he supported

TROUBLE IN NEW YORK

In 1863 Congress ordered a military draft in the North. Men could avoid being drafted by paying $300—a huge sum of money at the time. (A dollar in 1860 could buy about as much as $25 could today.) In July working men in New York City began to protest the law. They didn't want to join the Army, and they disliked the idea of the wealthy avoiding military service. The protest quickly turned into a riot.

Many of the rioters were Irish immigrants, and they soon turned their anger toward the city's African-Americans. The Irish saw free blacks as their competitors for unskilled jobs, and they opposed emancipation as a war aim. Army troops—some just back from the Battle of Gettysburg—arrived to end the violence, which lasted four days. Smaller riots broke out in other cities, but New York's was the worst, with more than 100 people killed.

the Confederacy. Throughout the Civil War, he showed great skill. But the North increasingly had more soldiers and more supplies, weakening Lee's chances for victory.

The successes at Vicksburg and Gettysburg established Union control of the Mississippi River and ended major southern campaigns in the North. Yet there was no doubt that many battles were still to come.

★THE STRUGGLE FOR CHATTANOOGA

During the weeks after Vicksburg fell, the Confederate state of Tennessee became a key battleground. Chattanooga, on the Tennessee River, was a major railway center. If the North controlled the region, it could use it as a base for attacks on Atlanta and other parts of Georgia. For the South, Chattanooga was a prime base for attacks on northern positions in western Tennessee and the border state of Kentucky.

The two sides first sent major armies to the region in June 1863. General William S. Rosecrans led 60,000 Union troops to the outskirts of Chattanooga. About 43,000 Confederate troops under General Braxton Bragg waited for the Yankees. In July the Union forces took control of Bragg's supply line, forcing him to take his army out of the city. Rosecrans marched his troops in, but Bragg received reinforcements and began a return march to Chattanooga.

In September the two armies clashed in northern Georgia along Chickamauga Creek. The battle on the first day, September 19, ended in a draw. On the second day, the South gained the advantage, though some of the greatest heroics came from General George H. Thomas, a Virginian who had remained loyal to the Union. When rebel troops smashed through a Union line, Thomas gathered his soldiers, who held off the

enemy with their bayo-
nets. For that, Thomas
earned the nickname
"The Rock of Chicka-
mauga," and he won
respect for his heroics at
other battles as well. Still
the Union forces had to
retreat, heading back
to Chattanooga. The
battle was an important
Confederate victory.

"The Rock of Chickamauga,"
General George H. Thomas

Now the South began its own siege. Bragg's troops
followed the Union forces to Chattanooga and seized most
of the supply routes into the city. Rosecrans would face
high casualties if he tried to leave. In October Lincoln put
Grant in charge of all Union forces in the West, which
included Tennessee. Grant then replaced Rosecrans with
Thomas as the commander in Chattanooga. Thomas
promised Grant, "We will hold the town until we starve."

Grant came to Chattanooga himself, and Union
reinforcements also began to arrive. General William
Tecumseh Sherman, one of Grant's best generals, led
some of the soldiers. Sherman, a retired soldier before the
war, had been living in Louisiana when that state seceded.
He moved north and rejoined the military after the attack

on Fort Sumter. In Tennessee Sherman and his men carved out a better supply route through the southern siege line. Then, as November went on, they prepared to leave the city and fight the Confederates.

The attack began November 23. Most of Bragg's men were positioned high above Chattanooga, on Missionary Ridge and Lookout Mountain. The main battles came the next two days, as Grant sent troops against each Confederate position. Lookout Mountain fell November 24, after a battle fought inside thick clouds. When the clouds parted late in the day, soldiers and residents in the valley could see the southerners retreating.

The next day Grant attacked Missionary Ridge from all sides. Thomas led the troops who had lost at

A Union general called the fighting at Lookout Mountain "the battle above the clouds."

Chickamauga, and they were eager to defeat Bragg's men this time. The soldiers were ordered to attack the first line of southern defense at the base of Missionary Ridge. But once they met their goal, they didn't stop. Grant watched in amazement as Thomas' men continued to scramble up the rocky ridge. No one had ordered the advance; the troops kept going on their own. They drove the Confederates off the ridge and sealed the victory at Chattanooga.

★A NEW COMMANDER

Chattanooga marked the last major battle for Grant and his army in 1863. President Lincoln took note of his impressive victories—and the Union's struggles closer to Washington, D.C. General George Meade had not been able to build on the North's victory at Gettysburg or weaken Lee's Army of Northern Virginia. Meade had first won fame at the Battle of Fredericksburg, leading Lincoln to make him commander of the Army of the Potomac. But Meade lost the president's confidence when he failed to attack Lee's retreating forces after the Battle of Gettysburg. When Lincoln learned that Meade had later let General James Longstreet's Confederate troops retreat safely from eastern Tennessee into western Virginia, the president exploded angrily: "Can anybody doubt if Grant were here in

General George Meade (center, with beard) and his staff in 1863

command that he would catch him?" Lincoln thought it was time to change the Union command structure. In March 1864 he named Ulysses S. Grant general in chief, commander of all Union forces.

Grant immediately set out a new plan for defeating the South. In the past Union forces had often focused on holding as much southern land as possible. Now Grant's goal would be to defeat the major southern armies on the battlefield. He knew that holding southern territory was a waste of time and men.

Grant put General Sherman in charge of all the Western troops, while he led the Army of the Potomac himself. Sherman focused first on the Army of Tennessee, now led by Confederate General Joseph Johnston, while Grant took on Lee's forces. Sherman also had another goal—to reach Atlanta, a railroad hub, and destroy the factories there. Without the supplies provided by the Georgia city, and the supply routes that ran through it, the Confederate army would begin to wither. Grant and Sherman now had a strategy. But they still faced a Confederacy convinced of the rightness of its cause, which Confederate President Jefferson Davis called "our holy struggle for liberty and independence." The Civil War was far from over.

QUANTRILL'S RAIDERS

The border state of Missouri had many pro-Confederate residents. The most notorious was William Quantrill. He led raids on Unionist civilians in Missouri and neighboring Kansas and also attacked Union troops. To some, Quantrill was more interested in stealing and carrying out revenge than helping the South. The war simply gave him an excuse. But some Missourians praised his attacks. In his deadliest assault, in August 1863, Quantrill and his raiders killed almost 200 Kansans. The North responded by forcing Missourians from their homes and letting pro-Union Kansans destroy the buildings. Quantrill finally moved on to other battlegrounds before his death in Kentucky in 1865. Four of his raiders who survived the war—Frank and Jesse James and Cole and Jim Younger—are best known today as famous outlaws of the Wild West.

CHAPTER 2
BATTLES IN VIRGINIA

Ulysses S. Grant took control of the Army of the Potomac in 1864 knowing he had the upper hand. The North was able to put more men in the field and could use a wide network of railways to transport men, weapons, and supplies. But Grant knew that to win the war, he had to destroy the forces of Robert E. Lee, a man he called "the acknowledged ablest general in the Confederate army."

Lee's army had spent the winter in Virginia low on food and supplies. He knew the advantages Grant had over him. Lee, though, could use the geography of Virginia to slow his enemy. The state's mountains, rivers, and forests made it hard for an army to advance against a foe dug in for defense. Lee's men were fiercely committed to their general and their cause. Sheer Union numbers would not scare them off.

As May began, Lee's army was camped along the Rapidan River, north of the Confederate capital of Richmond, Virginia. Nearby was a dense forested region called the

Wilderness. Grant moved his forces, about 120,000 men, south across the Rapidan, and on May 5 the Battle of the Wilderness began. The North's larger forces were slowed by the thick growth in the Wilderness. Artillery was almost useless. Lee attacked first, hoping to drive off the Union troops. Grant's men held firm. The next day Grant struck first, but the arrival of southern reinforcements ended his surge.

The clash in the Wilderness caused nearly 18,000 Union casualties, and Grant had no gains to show for it. The South's casualties were fewer than half that number. The fighting had set off fires in the woods that filled the air with thick smoke and killed any wounded who could not

The Battle of the Wilderness was the first major battle in Grant's Overland Campaign against Lee and the Army of Northern Virginia.

escape the flames. Grant said, "More desperate fighting has not been witnessed on this continent."

While the Battle of the Wilderness lasted just two days, the longer campaign stretched on for several more weeks. Unlike some northern commanders before him, Grant did not fall back after his losses. He wanted his larger force to keep pounding Lee's army. Grant pulled his men to the south and headed for the town of Spotsylvania Court House. Lee rushed his men there, arriving first, and the two armies fought again. The first skirmishes began May 8, with the main battle starting two days later. Some of the fiercest fighting came May 12, at a spot called the Bloody Angle. The Blue and Gray fought hand to hand, bayonets flashing as shots buzzed overhead. There was "a mass of torn and mutilated corpses," a Union officer later wrote. "Then fresh troops rushed madly forward to replace the dead, and so the murderous work went on." The South barely held off the swarming Union forces, and about 4,000 Confederates were taken as prisoners of war.

Grant and Lee fought throughout May, as Grant moved south and east in an attempt to get around Lee's army. The two sides fought a major battle June 3, at Cold Harbor, with heavy Union losses. Grant had about 13,000 casualties, compared with 2,500 for the South. But knowing that he outnumbered Lee, Grant moved on.

Union forces next crossed the James River and headed for Petersburg. Grant hoped to take the town and cut off supply routes to Richmond. Lee, however, was able to head off the northern troops, reaching the city first. Grant settled in for a siege of Petersburg. Lee prepared for it, but he knew time was against him. Grant had too many resources that he couldn't match.

THE BATTLE OF THE CRATER

During the Petersburg siege, some Union soldiers from Pennsylvania who had worked as coal miners created a plan to break through Confederate lines. They dug a shaft more than 500 feet (152 meters) long, then placed four tons of explosives under a southern artillery battery. The explosives' blast, on July 30, killed almost 300 Confederates and created a hole about 170 feet (52 m) long, 70 feet (21 m) wide, and 30 feet (9 m) deep. The two sides fought the Battle of the Crater around the hole. The Union fighters that day included a group of Ottawa and Chippewa Indian sharpshooters from Michigan. Despite the Indians' deadly aim, the northern forces did not do well because of poor leadership by Union generals. A soldier later wrote, "The old story again—a big slaughter, and nothing gained."

★FIGHTING TO THE WEST

The action in Virginia was not limited to the area around Richmond. In March Grant had ordered General Franz Sigel to prepare to move through the Shenandoah Valley. The valley in northwestern Virginia lies between the Allegheny and Blue Ridge mountain ranges. The rich farmland there provided food for the Confederates throughout the war. The scenery inspired a Union soldier who saw the valley to call it "a perfect paradise on earth." The valley also gave the South easy access to Washington, D.C., if they chose to use it.

Leading the Confederate forces was John C. Breckinridge. Just four years earlier, he had been vice president of the United States and a candidate for president. After losing to Lincoln, Breckinridge was elected a U.S. senator for the border state of Kentucky. But his vocal support for the Confederacy led to his leaving the Senate and the

John C. Breckinridge served as a Confederate general and secretary of war.

Union. He soon became a Confederate general. In May 1864 Breckinridge readied his defenses in the valley. They included about 300 teenagers from the nearby Virginia Military Institute (VMI), who were ready to put their education to use against the Yankee soldiers.

Sigel, meanwhile, marched south, and on May 15 his force met the Confederates at the small town of New Market. Breckinridge struck first from a well-defended position. Northern artillery began to strike their targets, but the Confederates slogged on through thick mud. The VMI cadets suffered heavy losses, with 55 casualties, including 10 deaths, but they fought bravely and helped keep the southern line intact. A Union cavalry charge ended badly, and the Confederates made one last, deadly thrust. A Union officer later remembered that "the rebels were coming on at the double-quick and concentrating their whole fire upon us. I told the men to run and get out of the fire as quickly as possible."

Despite the loss, the Union goal remained the same—destroy rail lines and take Staunton, a town at the end of the valley with important supply depots. After a victory outside the town, Union troops reached Staunton June 6. They moved from destroying army supplies to wrecking homes and businesses, and some soldiers even stole from the residents.

Union soldiers in a trench outside Petersburg in 1864

★THE SOUTH HITS BACK

General Lee decided to strike back. He sent General Jubal Early and 10,000 men to the valley. Early could be difficult to work with and was sometimes called Lee's "bad old man." But throughout the war he proved his bravery on the battlefield. Early's goal was to defend the town of Lynchburg, Virginia, just outside the valley, and drive back the Union troops. He was successful. Early and his soldiers then began to move down the valley. Their ultimate goal was to take Washington, D.C. Lee hoped a threat to the capital would force Grant to take troops away from the siege at Petersburg.

Early's men crossed the Potomac River July 5 and entered Union territory in Maryland. Near the Monocacy River, a small Union force prepared to meet Early's much larger army. Both Baltimore and Washington could fall if the Confederates kept advancing. By this time Grant had sent troops to help defend the capital. They reached the river July 8, a day before Early did. The Union defenses could not stop the rebels, but they slowed them enough for even more Union reinforcements to arrive. The new troops manned a series of forts that defended Washington.

On the morning of July 12, Early was near the city, close enough to see the dome of the U.S. Capitol. He also saw the reinforcements prepared to fight off his advance. Early sent out some skirmishers, but finally decided to pull back. He took some comfort in knowing he had "given the Federal authorities a terrible fright." He and his troops returned to Virginia. Washington was safe. And the war went on.

LINCOLN AT WAR

General Jubal Early's advance on Washington raised concerns for President Lincoln's safety. He left his summer home on the edge of the city and returned to the White House. The Navy readied a boat to whisk the Lincoln family out of the city, if necessary. On July 11, 1864, Lincoln was in one of the city's forts when the first of Early's forces arrived. Standing on a walkway near the top of the walls, the president was in clear view of the enemy, and his famous tall black hat made him an easy target. Lincoln finally left when a man near him was shot.

CHAPTER 3
SHERMAN ON THE MARCH

While Grant had prepared for his Virginia expedition against Lee, General Sherman had his own planning to do. His army numbered about 100,000, and his march from Chattanooga to Atlanta required a huge amount of supplies. He would also have to defend his supply line as he moved deeper into southern territory. So in April 1864 he sent 5,000 men to live in camps along 300 miles (483 kilometers) of railroad track. If the Confederates attacked the tracks, the workers could quickly rebuild them.

In his military training, Sherman had learned the traditional rules of war between two armies on a battlefield. During the Civil War, these rules had changed. He had seen a new kind of warfare developing. Civilians aided armies like never before in modern times, providing food and information or acting as guerrillas. Now Sherman prepared to introduce a new kind of fighting during his Georgia campaign—total war. Many civilians supported the Confederates and the war against the North. They would pay a price as well.

★INTO GEORGIA

By early May, Sherman's troops were camped just over the Tennessee border in northern Georgia. General Joseph Johnston's 65,000 Confederates were to the south, dug in at Dalton. Johnston had commanded troops in several earlier battles and once had been severely wounded. Now he had the task of slowing Sherman's advance.

Sherman drew out Johnston's troops by moving his men south to Resaca, where they had a better position. The two armies fought there from May 13 to May 16, suffering about equal losses. As the fighting ended, Johnston pulled back, as he would also do at future clashes between them. He knew he lacked the troops to directly attack Sherman. For now, he would have to take a defensive position. Sherman later wrote that Johnston was "claiming that he was purposely drawing us far from our base, and that when the right moment should come he would turn on us

William Tecumseh Sherman has been called the first modern general.

25

and destroy us. We were equally confident, and not the least alarmed."

Going into June, Sherman's progress was slow, with heavy rains and deep mud adding to his problems. On the other side, Johnston's men believed that their strategy of retreat might actually work. They were prepared to fight, and one confident soldier wrote in a letter home: "If they [Union troops] ever advance near here, they will certainly be the worst whipped set of men the sun ever shone on."

By mid-June, the Confederates were well positioned along a series of mountains outside Marietta, Georgia. After several days of skirmishing and artillery fire, Sherman launched a direct attack on Kennesaw Mountain. He had never tried to assault such well-defended lines before, and he never would again. The Battle of Kennesaw Mountain cost him 3,000 troops, three times the number of southern casualties.

But one Confederate victory did not change either side's plans. Sherman continually tried to take a position behind or to the side of the Confederates, where they would have to fight in the open. His troops also sought to control Johnston's supply line to Atlanta. On the other side, Johnston could not give up the supply line and he feared large losses in a direct battle. He continued to pull back.

Confederate artillery on Kennesaw Mountain rained shells down on Union troops as they prepared for an assault.

★ON TO ATLANTA

By midsummer, Sherman was only a few miles outside Atlanta. The citizens there removed supplies and machinery to keep the Yankees from getting them. Many fled the city. In the field, the two sides continued to fight, but Sherman was still not close to taking Atlanta. It was well-defended. Once again the North turned to a siege, cutting off supply routes into the city and winning several battles, further weakening the Confederate forces.

On August 7 Sherman wrote to Washington: "We keep hammering away all the time, and there is no

The Potter House in Atlanta was heavily damaged by Union shells in August 1864.

peace, inside or outside of Atlanta." Sherman brought in large cannons to shell the city. He assumed most civilians had left, but about 10,000 people were still there. They sought shelter from the shells, some taking cover in what they called "gopher holes." These were crude bomb shelters with pieces of wood over the hole and dirt on top of the wood. A Confederate nurse described the fear of the women and children: They "trembled and hungered and thirsted in their underground places of refuge while the earth above them shook with constant explosions."

Sherman made his final move August 28, swinging south of Atlanta. His men began to destroy the last rail lines carrying supplies. The Confederates, now under

THE BATTLE OF MOBILE BAY

As General William T. Sherman headed to Atlanta, the Union Navy won a key victory at Mobile, Alabama. Since the beginning of the war, the Navy had maintained a blockade of southern ports along the Atlantic Ocean and the Gulf Coast. This greatly reduced the South's ability to ship cotton to market and to receive goods and weapons. Mobile was a port for many ships that broke through the Union blockade.

In August 1864 the powerful new ironclad *Tennessee* was in Mobile, preparing for its first voyages. Union Admiral David Farragut decided to attack the *Tennessee* before it could reach the sea. On August 5 Farragut led a small fleet into Mobile Bay, which was filled with explosive mines, then called torpedoes. Shells filled the sky as Union ships sped past Confederate forts at Farragut's famous order: "Damn the torpedoes! Full speed ahead." The northern ships heavily damaged the *Tennessee* and other Confederate vessels. Farragut's victory shut down the port, reducing the South's ability to avoid the northern blockade.

the command of General John B. Hood, tried to fight the Union forces, but his men were split and were no match for the northerners. The last Confederate forces left Atlanta, and on September 2 the first Union troops marched in.

★NEW PLANS

With Grant making no progress in Virginia, Sherman's capture of Atlanta boosted spirits in the North. The city itself, though, presented a depressing sight. Buildings were burned or destroyed, and looters stole what they could. The residents, unsure how they would be treated, feared the Yankees entering the city. They were thankful that Union troops restored order, though, and soon shops began reopening.

Sherman dealt with Hood's remaining army. The Confederates tried to cut the Union supply lines into the city. Sherman sent thousands of troops to track them down, and the two armies fought in northern Georgia. By late October, Hood had another plan—move through Alabama and challenge Union troops based in Tennessee. He hoped the invasion would force Sherman to leave Atlanta and fight him. If Sherman didn't follow, then perhaps Hood could retake Tennessee and use it as a base for attacks on Kentucky.

Sherman, however, no longer wanted to defeat Hood. He wanted to smash the southern will to fight. A march to the sea, through an undefended Georgia, would do it. The march would also destroy more railways and supplies that otherwise could help the southern war effort.

Sherman's troops tore up railroads as they marched through Georgia to the sea.

Sherman sent some men after Hood, but 62,000 remained with him in Atlanta. The Blue and Gray fought major battles at Franklin and Nashville, Tennessee, but by the end of the year the Confederate threat in that state had ended. Sherman's troops began leaving Atlanta November 15, 1864. They had burned any remaining buildings that might have military use. The fires had quickly spread, reducing most of Atlanta to ashes. A Union officer later wrote that there were "vast waves and sheets of flames thrusting themselves heavenward," calling it a "grand but awful sight." To the remaining Atlantans, it was merely awful.

Sherman's first goal was Milledgeville, then the capital of Georgia. The state's government required all white males 16 to 55 years old to join the military and try to stop the Union advance. Sherman's men met defenders along the way, but the Union troops soon overpowered the mixture of militia and Confederate soldiers. They also came across slaves, who were happy to see troops in blue. Their arrival meant the enslaved people finally had their freedom. Some had managed to escape as their owners prepared to flee; some simply had been left behind. Many blacks joined Sherman's line of troops, and some worked for the Union Army. Others were caught by the Confederates. Some of them were killed, and others were forced to return to their masters.

★ON TO SAVANNAH

Union forces reached Milledgeville November 23, then headed for the coastal city of Savannah. Sherman wrote that "the first stage of the journey was, therefore, complete, and absolutely successful." His men lived off the land, taking the crops and meat they needed from nearby farms. They burned plantations of owners who had been strong supporters of the Confederacy. At times, the Union troops killed farm animals they could not take with them, just so the local people could not eat them. The harsh treatment stirred southern anger, but the Georgians could not stop Sherman and his men. A Union major said that Sherman's "total war" was the only way to win: "It must make the innocent suffer as well as the guilty."

By December 9, Sherman's army was just outside Savannah. A Confederate force of about 10,000 men had gathered to defend the city. They held off the Yankee invaders for several days. But Union ships were bringing supplies and artillery to Sherman, and Savannah could not survive a full assault. The Confederate troops managed to pull out of the

THE BUMMERS

General Sherman set down strict rules for foraging—taking food and supplies from farms. But over time, some of Sherman's soldiers foraged largely on their own and took whatever they wanted. They became known as bummers. First working on foot, they later took horses from nearby farms and formed a sort of cavalry unit. Some of the bummers were soldiers who had left their own units, preferring to forage rather than fight. Even Confederate deserters and civilians joined the groups. The bummers did more than steal—at times they burned property as well. Sherman eventually put officers in charge of the bummers to stop the worst of their actions.

Sherman and his Union troops entered Savannah just before Christmas 1864.

city before a major battle, and Sherman marched in December 23. He sent a message to President Lincoln: "I beg to present you as a Christmas gift the city of Savannah."

The Civil War had dragged on for nearly four years, but Sherman's success offered the Union hope for 1865.

CHAPTER 4
OFF THE BATTLEFIELD

Military campaigns were not the North's only focus during the fall of 1864. Abraham Lincoln was running for his second term as president, and he faced his own hard-fought battle. Lincoln was not popular all across the Union. His critics included Democrats who had opposed the war from the start and people who disliked the Emancipation Proclamation. Even some Republicans, members of his own party, weren't happy with him. They thought he had waited too long to end slavery and hadn't gone far enough, since it still existed in some of the border states.

Democrats thought Lincoln had used the war to take more power than the Constitution allowed. They attacked "the arbitrary [random and unfair] military arrest, imprisonment, trial, and sentence of American citizens in States where civil law exists in full force; the suppression of freedom of speech and of the press … [and] open and avowed disregard of State rights." The Democrats chose General George McClellan as their presidential candidate. McClellan had left the Union Army in 1862, after several disagreements with Lincoln over how to fight the war. McClellan and the Democrats now wanted to end the war, allow the South to return to the Union, and let southern states keep slavery. McClellan counted on votes from Americans tired of the war.

Democrat George McClellan and his running mate, George H. Pendleton

Sherman's victory in Atlanta helped Lincoln's chances to defeat McClellan. So did gains in the Shenandoah Valley, where General Philip Sheridan now led northern troops. Sheridan had commanded both foot soldiers and cavalry troops with equal success. His victories against Jubal Early ended the threat that Confederates would once again move up the valley to attack the North. With increasing hope for soon defeating the South, northerners stuck with Lincoln. The president won 55 percent of the popular vote and was favored in all but three of the 25 Union states. Lincoln also won the votes of most Union soldiers in the field. Sensing victory was close, they wanted to support their commander in chief. After his victory, he asked members of both parties to "reunite in a common effort to save our common country."

Lincoln's victory affected the South as much as the North. If McClellan had been elected, he would have sought to end the war peacefully and allow slavery to continue. Lincoln, the Confederates knew, would keep fighting until he had forced them to surrender on his terms. The recent losses on the battlefield and Lincoln's win at the polls offered the South little hope for victory as 1864 came to an end.

★WOUNDED AND CAPTURED

On both sides, the battle losses included hundreds of thousands of wounded soldiers. Women in both the North and South played an important role in military hospitals. They took care of the sick and injured, trying to heal their battered spirits as well as their bodies. A southern nurse said, "I have never worked so hard in all my life and I would rather do that than anything else in the world." The war helped make women a key part of nursing. Before the war, most nurses were men. Since so many men went to fight, women had to help in hospitals.

While some soldiers left the battlefield because of their injuries, others were taken away as prisoners of war. In the first two years of the war, the North and South usually exchanged their prisoners soon after a battle. Some prisoners were allowed to go home, as long as they promised not to fight again until the two sides made a formal prisoner exchange. The situation changed when the North began using African-American troops. The South did not consider them soldiers and would not exchange northern prisoners for them. Later, General Grant opposed the exchanges. He was taking large numbers of Confederate prisoners and did

Southern prisoners were usually allowed to keep their canteens, blankets, and haversacks.

not want them to be released to fight again. The North had more troops, so it didn't need its prisoners back as badly as the South did.

Both sides built large prisoner-of-war camps to hold captured enemy soldiers. During the war, the North captured about 215,000 southerners, while the Confederacy had almost 195,000 Union prisoners. The prison camps were usually bleak, crowded, and dirty. The worst camps included Andersonville in Georgia, Libby Prison in Richmond, Camp Douglas in Illinois,

ANDERSONVILLE

Of all the prisoner-of-war camps, Andersonville was the worst. It opened early in 1864, and by that summer almost 33,000 Union men were there—three times as many as the camp was supposed to hold. A total of 50,000 prisoners passed through the camp, and almost one-third of them died. An intestinal illness called dysentery caused many of the deaths, and a priest who visited the camp said that at times 150 men died every day. After the war, the U.S. government arrested the camp's commander, Captain Henry Wirz. The captain was executed for war crimes—he had made decisions that had increased the suffering and death rate of Union prisoners.

and Fort Delaware, on an island in the Delaware River. Tens of thousands of prisoners died at these and other camps, mostly from illness or a lack of food. At times, though, guards killed prisoners who disobeyed orders.

A northern prisoner later wrote that at his camp, the men slept on "a strip of the bare, hard floor, about six feet by two." A southerner at Fort Delaware wrote about receiving water that was a salty, clouded "fluid scarcely one whit better than the water from the Delaware, which oozes through the ditches in the pen." Despite harsh conditions, the prisoners tried to stay busy. A visiting minister might bring books or magazines to read. Some prisoners played cards or checkers, while others carved things out of bone or wood. They often traded them with other prisoners or their guards in return for tobacco or extra food.

★A TRUE END TO SLAVERY

In January 1865 Abraham Lincoln was waiting to be sworn in for his second term as president. Although he had battled with Congress in the past, he managed to get the lawmakers to take an important step. On January 31 the House of Representatives voted for the 13th Amendment to the Constitution. The Senate had already passed the measure, and now the states would

The House of Representatives voted 119 to 56 in favor of the 13th Amendment, which abolished slavery.

consider whether to ratify it. The amendment abolished slavery across the entire United States. Lincoln also proposed requiring southern states wishing to rejoin the Union to first ratify the amendment, and Congress agreed. When the war began, Lincoln had not said he wanted to end slavery, but the war's severity and death toll, among other things, had changed his mind.

Now the war would achieve that goal—if the Union could win.

CHAPTER 5
VICTORY AND LOSS

Through the fall and winter of 1864, General Grant monitored events across the country. General Sherman marched through Georgia, Lincoln won re-election, and the Confederates made their last stand in Tennessee. But in Petersburg, Virginia, the siege went on. The armies exchanged rifle shots and artillery fire, but no major battles erupted. Grant was waiting for General Lee to make a move, and Lee was not ready to do anything.

Lee knew he faced an almost impossible situation. In the fall, he wrote his wife, Mary Anna, "The enemy is very numerous & still increasing & is able by his superiority of numbers to move at pleasure." The Confederates could not disrupt the Union supply lines, so plenty of food reached the growing Northern army. Meanwhile, in Petersburg, Lee's men faced food shortages, with one soldier complaining, "I can eat three times what I get for we only get anuft [enough] for one meal in twenty four hours."

By January 1865, Lee was seeing more of his men

Hungry Confederate soldiers chased a rabbit through camp.

desert, adding to his problems. The deserters ached for food, or were merely tired of the war. Above all, many left to protect their loved ones at home. They knew about the difficulties civilians faced, with food supplies low and the threat of Union attack. Lee became so desperate to increase his numbers that he asked to be allowed to recruit slaves as soldiers. This appalled and frightened many Confederates, and he did not get permission until the war's last weeks. The war ended before any enslaved men could be trained or put into battle for the Confederacy.

★LAST STAB AT VICTORY

Hundreds of miles south of Petersburg, Sherman had continued his march northward, through South Carolina. His goal was to join with Grant's forces. In March General Sheridan was on his way from the Shenandoah Valley to do the same thing. Lee had only one hope to save his army: break out of Petersburg and head west and then south. There he could meet General Johnston, who was trying to stop Sherman. If the combined southern forces defeated Sherman, they could then swing north to take on Grant.

Lee faced a Union line almost 40 miles (64 km) long, curving from near Richmond down around Petersburg. His first goal was to strike with a quick, hard thrust at the Union supply lines. If they were cut, some of the northern troops would have to retreat, giving Lee a chance to leave Petersburg.

On March 25 General John B. Gordon led the first Confederate assault. His target was Fort Stedman, not far from the railway. His troops moved out before dawn, storming out of trenches the South had built as part of its defenses. The Confederates soon overwhelmed the outnumbered Union troops at Stedman. But as the sun rose, Union artillery blasted the fort, and the North soon retook it. Grant's men were even able to capture land the Confederates had held. The Confederate plan had failed.

Abraham Lincoln discussed peace plans with (from left) Generals William T. Sherman and Ulysses S. Grant and Admiral David Porter.

Two days later President Lincoln met with Grant, Sherman, and Admiral David D. Porter at City Point, Virginia, near Petersburg. The men knew that Lee and his army were doomed. The Union leaders, who met aboard a boat called *River Queen*, discussed what to do when the Union finally had its victory. Lincoln said they should not punish the captured southerners: "We want those people to return to their allegiance to the Union and submit to the laws."

Soon Grant made his own move to cut off supply lines and to force Lee's army out of its trenches. Grant sent infantry and cavalry under Sheridan's command

SEEKING TO HEAL

Even before meeting General Grant in Virginia, President Lincoln had shown his desire for a fair peace. His goal was to heal the nation after its painful division. He expressed that message in one of his most famous speeches, his second Inaugural Address, on March 4, 1865. These words from that speech are carved into a wall of the Lincoln Memorial in Washington, D.C.: "With malice toward none; with charity for all; with firmness in the right, as God gives us to see the right, let us strive on to finish the work we are in; to bind up the nation's wounds; to care for him who shall have borne the battle, and for his widow, and his orphan—to do all which may achieve and cherish a just and a lasting peace, among ourselves, and with all nations."

to an area southwest of Petersburg, near the main Confederate railway. On April 1, at Five Forks, Sheridan's forces defeated southern troops led by General George Pickett, one of the South's heroes at Gettysburg. Sheridan took about 4,500 prisoners, and Lee's army was down to about 30,000 men. Grant had four times as many under his command.

★THE ROAD TO APPOMATTOX

Grant struck again the next day, hitting the main Confederate lines. In some battles, the southerners used all their bullets and fought the advancing enemy with their bayonets, clubs, and even rocks. But the North could not be stopped. That evening Lee ordered his men to pull out of both Richmond and Petersburg and retreat west.

Over the next several days, the North pressed on. Grant's forces soon took Richmond, reaching it after Confederates had burned supplies stored there. Fires started by retreating Confederates and arriving Union

Much of Richmond was in ruins after fires roared through the Confederate capital.

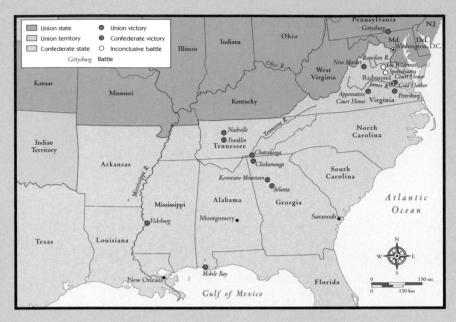

After the Confederate defeat at Gettysburg, all remaining major Civil War battles were fought in the South.

soldiers spread throughout the city, creating what a local newspaper called "a sea of fire." Meanwhile, the larger part of the Union Army chased Lee, trying to cut off his escape. Union cavalrymen rode past the rebel soldiers, cutting them down. Blue-coated infantrymen destroyed Confederate supply wagons and captured prisoners. Watching the Battle of Sayler's Creek from a hill, Lee said, "That half of our army is destroyed."

On April 9 near the town of Appomattox Court House, Lee tried one last attack. Sheridan had raced ahead of him. General Gordon led a Confederate advance. When the attack failed, Lee agreed to meet with Grant and surrender his army. For the meeting,

General Lee (seated, left) surrendered to General Grant (seated, center) at the home of Wilmer McLean in Appomatox Court House, Virginia.

Grant wore a worn and muddy blue uniform. Lee's gray uniform was new—he wanted to look his best if he was going to be taken prisoner.

The two men chatted politely, then got down to business. Grant followed Lincoln's order to treat the defeated enemy well. Lee's men would be allowed to go home and take their private property. Grant would also provide food. Grant later wrote that he was not happy watching Lee surrender. He considered Lee and his men "a foe who had fought so long and valiantly, and had suffered so much." But Grant was glad the war was almost over.

★NEWS OF VICTORY—AND DEFEAT

President Lincoln soon learned of Lee's surrender. The next morning hundreds of cannons fired in Washington to announce the Union triumph. Gideon Welles, a member of Lincoln's Cabinet, wrote, "Guns are firing, bells ringing, flags flying, men laughing, children cheering, all, all jubilant." Similar celebrations soon broke out across the North. On April 11 Lincoln spoke to a crowd that had gathered outside the White House. He said he hoped for a "speedy peace" but warned that bringing the South back into the Union would not be easy, since "we … differ among ourselves as to the mode, manner, and means of reconstruction."

In the South, however, the reaction was very different. People cried when they heard Lee had surrendered. Some refused to believe it. A woman who had left

After the war Robert E. Lee became president of Washington College (now Washington and Lee University) in Lexington, Virginia.

President Lincoln had freed southern slaves with the Emancipation Proclamation, but it took the presence of Union troops to enforce it. In Texas word of the end of slavery did not come until June 19, 1865. With the war over, Union General Gordon Granger arrived with several thousand troops and announced that slavery had been abolished. At the time Texas still had 250,000 slaves. Within two years, free blacks in Texas were celebrating June 19 as a holiday now called Juneteenth. African-Americans and others across the country still celebrate Juneteenth to mark the end of slavery in the United States.

her family's plantation in Louisiana to seek refuge in Texas wrote in her journal, "I cannot bear to hear them talk of defeat."

Jefferson Davis and his Cabinet had fled Richmond a week earlier. The Confederate president was not ready to give up. The North was taking control of major cities in the Deep South, he knew, but the Confederates still had an army west of the Mississippi River. Davis hoped he and his Cabinet could flee there and continue the fight. He never made it. Davis was captured in Georgia May 10.

After the surrender at Appomattox, most southerners realized that talk of continuing the war was useless. The

A Confederate soldier was among the more than 620,000 who died during the Civil War.

North had won. Slavery had ended. The country would now focus on reconstruction. The South would have to be rebuilt. The factories, railroads, and farms destroyed by war would have to be rebuilt. The Union also would have to recover. The North and South had to find a way to work together again as a united nation.

One thing they shared was the huge amount of suffering the war had brought. More than 620,000 American soldiers, from both the North and South, had died during the war, many from disease. Hundreds of thousands of others had been wounded and survived, although tens of thousands of them had lost arms or legs. In the South, thousands of civilians had starved to death.

★A PAINFUL LOSS

President Lincoln had been thinking about reconstruction for several years. Throughout 1864 he had argued with Congress on the details of a plan. Now, with the war over, Lincoln hoped to take action. But a night at the theater changed everything.

On April 14 Lincoln and his wife, Mary, went to Washington's Ford's Theatre. A popular comedy was playing. As the crowd enjoyed the show, a man crept into the private box where Lincoln sat. He fired a single bullet into the president's head. Then the assassin, John Wilkes Booth, fled the theater.

John Wilkes Booth was tracked down and killed by Union soldiers 12 days after he assassinated President Lincoln.

Booth, a well-known actor, had supported the Confederacy and hated Lincoln. He had recruited several people to help him kidnap the president, but then decided to kill him instead. The plot also included killing several members of Lincoln's Cabinet. Those efforts failed, but Booth's didn't. As Booth made his escape, Lincoln lay dying in the theater.

The president was quickly moved to a building across the street. As his Cabinet members gathered there, a doctor tried to save him, but there was nothing he could do. On the morning of April 15, Lincoln died. The joyous mood in the North after Grant's victory soon turned to deep sadness. The nation's African-Americans were especially affected. To them, Lincoln was the Great Emancipator, the man who had given them their freedom.

After a service in Washington, D.C., Lincoln's body was taken back to his hometown of Springfield, Illinois. During the nearly two-week journey on the funeral train and in the weeks that followed, more than a million Americans paid their respects to the dead president. Sidney Fisher of Philadelphia was one of them. He said what many Americans must have felt: "I feel as tho' I had lost a personal friend."

Lincoln refused to let the South secede. He fought the Civil War to keep the Union whole. His actions

A funeral train carried Abraham Lincoln's body from Washington, D.C., to Springfield, Illinois, for burial.

angered many Americans, and the war cost a great many lives. Yet Lincoln reached his goal, and ended slavery as well.

Now a new president would step forward to lead the nation during Reconstruction. With Lincoln's death, Vice President Andrew Johnson took over the presidency. The war was over, but the country still faced many difficult years as it tried to become whole again.

TIMELINE

May: Union attack on Vicksburg, Mississippi, fails and General Ulysses S. Grant begins a siege of the city

July: Vicksburg surrenders; Union forces win a huge battle at Gettysburg, in Pennsylvania; New York City draft riots erupt

September: South wins the Battle of Chickamauga, in northern Georgia

November: North breaks the Confederate siege of Chattanooga

May: General Robert E. Lee's forces inflict heavy Union casualties at the Battle of the Wilderness, in Virginia; fierce fighting erupts at the Bloody Angle during the Battle of Spotsylvania Court House, where both sides have high losses; Union and Confederate forces suffer almost equal losses at the Battle of Resaca, in northern Georgia; in the Shenandoah Valley, the South wins the Battle of New Market

June: Union troops under General David Hunter destroy large parts of Staunton, Virginia; Grant begins a siege of Petersburg

July: Confederate forces under General Jubal Early threaten Washington, D.C., but are forced to retreat; at Petersburg, the Battle of the Crater takes place around a huge hole created by Union explosives

August: Admiral David Farragut leads the Union Navy to victory at Mobile Bay, Alabama

September: Sherman's forces enter Atlanta

November: Abraham Lincoln wins his second term as president; Sherman reaches the Georgia capital of Milledgeville on his way to the sea

December: Sherman takes Savannah

January: Congress approves the 13th Amendment to the Constitution, which outlaws slavery

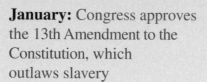

March: President Lincoln gives his second Inaugural Address, urging Americans to heal the divided nation; Lee's forces fail to break through the Union siege at Petersburg

April: Union General Philip Sheridan wins the Battle of Five Forks; Lee orders a Confederate retreat from Petersburg and Richmond; after an unsuccessful attack at Appomattox Court House, Lee surrenders to Grant; President Lincoln is shot at Washington's Ford's Theatre and dies; Andrew Johnson becomes president

May: Confederate President Jefferson Davis is arrested in Georgia

June: The last slaves in Texas learn they are free

December: The 13th Amendment to the Constitution is ratified by the states

GLOSSARY

artillery: large guns, such as cannons

assassin: person who kills an important or well-known figure, such as a political leader

battery: group or unit of cannons and the men operating them

blockade: naval action to prevent ships from entering or leaving a port

border states: during the Civil War, the slave states along the border of the North and South—Delaware, Kentucky, Maryland, and Missouri—that remained in the Union

Cabinet: heads of government departments who also advise the president

campaign: series of battles carried out by one army

candidate: person running for political office

casualties: people killed or wounded during a conflict; in a war, also includes soldiers captured or missing

cavalry: soldiers who fight on horseback

depots: buildings where military supplies are stored

desert: leave a military unit without permission and without plans to return

draft:	system for staffing the military that forces civilians to join the army
emancipation:	the act of freeing someone or a group from bondage
guerrillas:	fighters not part of a regular army who strike quickly, then hide
haversack:	bag similar to a knapsack but worn over one shoulder
infantry:	soldiers who fight on foot
ironclad:	ship made of wood covered with metal
malice:	desire to cause pain or distress
militia:	citizens who train as soldiers and fight as needed during emergencies
reinforcements:	extra troops sent to help an army already in the field
sharpshooter:	soldier trained to accurately fire a gun over long distances
shell:	metal container filled with gunpowder and fired from a cannon
siege:	surrounding of a town to cut off the entry of supplies and force its surrender
skirmishes:	exchanges of gunfire between small groups of soldiers, often before a major battle

ADDITIONAL RESOURCES

FURTHER READING

Beller, Susan Provost. *Billy Yank and Johnny Reb: Soldiering in the Civil War.* Minneapolis: Twenty-First Century Books, 2008.

Chorlian, Meg, ed. *Ulysses S. Grant: Unlikely Hero of the Civil War.* Peterborough, N.H.: Cobblestone Publishing, 2006.

Fradin, Dennis Brindell. *The Assassination of Abraham Lincoln.* New York: Benchmark Books, 2006.

Santella, Andrew. *Surrender at Appomattox.* Minneapolis: Compass Point Books, 2006.

Swanson, James L. *Chasing Lincoln's Killer.* New York: Scholastic Press, 2009.

Warren, Andrea. *Under Siege: Three Children at the Civil War Battle for Vicksburg.* New York: Melanie Kroupa Books, 2009.

INTERNET SITES

Use FactHound to find Internet sites related to this book. All of the sites on FactHound have been researched by our staff.

Here's all you do:

Visit *www.facthound.com*

Type in this code: 9780756543693

Read all the books in the Civil War series:

A Nation Divided: The Long Road to the Civil War

Bull Run to Gettysburg: Early Battles of the Civil War

North Over South: Final Victory in the Civil War

Reconstruction: Rebuilding America after the Civil War

SELECT BIBLIOGRAPHY

Andrews, Peter. "The Rock of Chickamauga." *American Heritage.* March 1990. 22 March 2010. www.americanheritage.com/articles/magazine/ah/1990/2/1990_2_81.shtml

Catton, Bruce. *The American Heritage New History of the Civil War.* Edited by James M. McPherson. New York: Viking Penguin, 1996.

Commager, Henry Steele, ed. *Living History: The Civil War.* Revised and expanded by Erik Bruun. New York: Ten Press, 2000.

Confederate Industry: Manufacturers and Quartermasters in the Civil War by Harold S. Wilson. Book review by David Surdam. September 2002. 22 March 2010. http://eh.net/bookreviews/library/0543

Dammann, Gordon, and Alfred J. Bollet. *Images of Civil War Medicine: A Photographic History.* New York: Demos Medical Publishing, 2007.

Donald, David Herbert. *Lincoln.* New York: Simon & Schuster, 1995.

Fowler, William M. Jr. *Under Two Flags: The American Navy in the Civil War.* Annapolis, Md.: Bluejacket Books, 1990.

Gienapp, William E. *Abraham Lincoln and the Civil War.* New York: Oxford University Press, 2002.

Glatthaar, Joseph J. *General Lee's Army: From Victory to Collapse.* New York: Free Press, 2008.

Grant, Ulysses S. *Personal Memoirs of U.S. Grant.* Vol. II. New York: Charles L. Webster and Company, 1885. 22 March 2010. http://lincoln.lib.niu.edu/cgi-bin/philologic/getobject.pl?c.4513:9.lincoln

Harwell, Richard B., ed. *The Confederate Reader.* New York: Longman's Green and Co., 1957.

Heidler, David Stephen, Jeanne T. Heidler, and David J. Coles, eds. *Encyclopedia of the American Civil War: A Political, Social, and Military History.* New York: W.W. Norton & Company, 2002.

Hofstadter, Richard, and Michael Wallace, eds. *American Violence: A Documentary History.* New York: Vintage, 1970.

Lepa, Jack H. *Breaking the Confederacy: The Georgia and Tennessee Campaigns of 1864.* Jefferson, N.C.: McFarland & Co., 2005.

Lepa, Jack H. *The Shenandoah Valley Campaign of 1864.* Jefferson, N.C.: McFarland & Co., 2003.

"Life and Death in the White House." The American Presidency. National Museum of American History. 22 March 2010. http://american history.si.edu/Presidency/3d1a4.html

McPherson, James. *Battle Cry of Freedom: The Civil War Era.* New York: Oxford University Press, 2003.

Mosier, John. *Grant: A Biography.* New York: Palgrave Macmillan, 2006.

Rasmussen, William M.S., and Robert S. Tilton. *Lee and Grant.* Richmond: Virginia Historical Society, 2007.

Shenandoah at War. 22 March 2010. www.shenandoahatwar.org/index.php

Trudeau, Noah Andre. *Southern Storm: Sherman's March to the Sea.* New York: Harper, 2008.

The West. William Clarke Quantrill. 22 March 2010. www.pbs.org/weta/thewest/people/i_r/quantrill.htm

SOURCE NOTES

Page 5, line 15: Vicksburg National Military Park: Vicksburg is the Key! 22 March 2010. https://sercms.nps.gov/vick/historyculture/vickkey.htm

Page 7, line 11: Henry Steele Commager, ed. *Living History: The Civil War.* Revised and expanded by Erik Bruun. New York: Ten Press, 2000, p. 475.

Page 8, line 4: Ibid., p. 480.

Page 9, sidebar, line 3: Scott Derks. *The Value of a Dollar: Prices and Incomes in the United States, 1860–2009.* Millerton, N.Y.: Grey House Publishing, 2009, p. xix.

Page 11, line 20: Bruce Catton. *The American Heritage New History of the Civil War.* Edited by James M. McPherson. New York: Viking Penguin, 1996, p. 392.

Page 13, line 24: David Herbert Donald. *Lincoln.* New York: Simon & Schuster, 1995, p. 490.

Page 15, line 7: Richard B. Harwell, ed. *The Confederate Reader.* New York: Longman's Green and Company, 1957, p. 252.

Page 16, line 6: Ulysses S. Grant. *Personal Memoirs of U.S. Grant.* Vol. II. New York: Charles L. Webster and Company, 1885, p. 126. 22 March 2010. http://lincoln.lib.niu.edu/cgi-bin/philologic/getobject.pl?c.4513:9.lincoln

Page 18, line 1: William M.S. Rasmussen and Robert S. Tilton. *Lee and Grant.* Richmond: Virginia Historical Society, 2007, p. 212.

Page 18, line 15: *Living History: The Civil War,* p. 736.

Page 19, sidebar, line 15: *The American Heritage New History of the Civil War,* p. 434.

Page 20, line 8: Jack H. Lepa. *The Shenandoah Valley Campaign of 1864.* Jefferson, N.C.: McFarland & Company, 2003, p. 13.

Page 21, line 15: *Col. George D. Wells' Official Report for the Battle of New Market.* May 15, 1864. 22 March 2010. www.civilwarhome.com/wellsnewmarket.htm

Page 23, line11: *The Shenandoah Valley Campaign of 1864,* p. 113.

Page 25, line 21: *Living History: The Civil War,* p. 698.

Page 26, line 8: Jack H. Lepa. *Breaking the Confederacy: The Georgia and Tennessee Campaigns of 1864.* Jefferson, N.C.: McFarland & Company, 2005, p. 57.

Page 27, line 10: Ibid., p. 106.

Page 28, line 9: Ibid., p. 108.

Page 29, sidebar, line 16: James McPherson. *Battle Cry of Freedom: The Civil War Era.* New York: Oxford University Press, 2003, p. 761.

Page 31, line 9: Noah Andre Trudeau. *Southern Storm: Sherman's March to the Sea.* New York: Harper, 2008, p. 68.

Page 32, line 18: Ibid., p. 218.

Page 33, line 4: *Breaking the Confederacy: The Georgia and Tennessee Campaigns of 1864,* p. 158.

Page 34, line 3: *Lincoln,* p. 553.

Page 35, line 13: "Democratic Party Platform, 1864." 22 March 2010. www.sewanee.edu/Faculty/Willis/Civil_War/documents/democratic.html

Page 37, line 5: *Lincoln,* p. 546.

Page 37, line 21: *The American Heritage New History of the Civil War,* p. 364.

Page 40, line 6: *Living History: The Civil War,* p. 492.

Page 40, line 8: Ibid., p. 498.

Page 42, line 10: *Lee and Grant,* p. 218.

Page 42, line 16: Joseph J. Glatthaar. *General Lee's Army: From Victory to Collapse.* New York: Free Press, 2008, p. 437.

Page 45, line 7: *Lee and Grant*, p. 220.

Page 46, sidebar, line 7: Abraham Lincoln's Second Inaugural Address. 22 March 2010. http://showcase.netins.net/web/creative/lincoln/speeches/inaug2.htm

Page 48, line 2: Civil War Richmond. From the *Richmond Whig*. 4 April 1865. 22 March 2010. www.mdgorman.com/Written_Accounts/Whig/1865/richmond_whig_441865.htm

Page 48, line 8: *The American Heritage New History of the Civil War*, p. 566.

Page 49, line 9: *Personal Memoirs of U.S. Grant*, p. 489. 23 April 2010. http://lincoln.lib.niu.edu/cgi-bin/philologic/getobject.pl?c.4513:29.lincoln

Page 50, line 4: *Lincoln*, p. 581.

Page 50, line 13: Ibid., p. 582.

Page 51, line 2: *General Lee's Army: From Victory to Collapse*, p. 471.

Page 52, line 8: *Battle Cry of Freedom: The Civil War Era*, p. 854.

Page 54, line 23: "Life and Death in the White House." The American Presidency. National Museum of American History. 22 March 2010. http://americanhistory.si.edu/Presidency/3d1a4.html

INDEX

ABOUT THE AUTHOR

Michael Burgan is a freelance writer of books for children and adults. A history graduate of the University of Connecticut, he has written more than 200 fiction and nonfiction children's books. For adult audiences, he has written news articles, essays, and plays. Burgan is a recipient of an Educational Press Association of America award.